People of the Arctic

by Betsy Hebert

Scott Foresman
is an imprint of

Glenview, Illinois • Boston, Massachusetts • Mesa, Arizona
Shoreview, Minnesota • Upper Saddle River, New Jersey

Illustrator 3 Dan Trush

Photographs
Every effort has been made to secure permission and provide appropriate credit for photographic material. The publisher deeply regrets any omission and pledges to correct errors called to its attention in subsequent editions.

Unless otherwise acknowledged, all photographs are the property of Pearson Education, Inc.

Photo locators denoted as follows: Top (T), Center (C), Bottom (B), Left (L), Right (R), Background (Bkgd)

CVR © Galen Rowell/Corbis; **1** © Galen Rowell/Corbis; **4** Brandon Cole/Jupiter Images; **5** Cindy Miller Hopkins/Danita Delimont Agency/Digital Railroad; **6** © Bryan & Cherry Alexander Photography/Alamy Images; **7** © Vincent Lowe/Alamy Images; **8** © blickwinkel /Alamy Images; **9** © Eastcott/Momatiuk/The Image Works, Inc.; **10** © tbkmedia.de /Alamy Images; **11** Staffan Widstrand/Corbis; **12** © Galen Rowell/Corbis

ISBN 13: 978-0-328- 39412-8
ISBN 10:   0-328- 39412-2

The Arctic is the area around the North
Pole. The air in the Arctic is always cold,
and there is lots of ice and snow

This map shows the Arctic region.

But there is life in the Arctic. Willow trees and grasses grow. Polar bears and other animals live there. Seals and fish swim and twitch in the water.

People live in the Arctic too. The Inuit
people have lived there for thousands of years.

The Inuit know the winter is long and cold. They work hard to get ready for cold weather.

First, an Inuit family hunts and fishes throughout the summer. They eat some of the food.

Next, they dry some of the food and save it for winter.

Last, the family moves into a winter home that is made of wood or stone.

In the summer, the family might live in a tent, but a tent won't keep them warm during the cold Arctic winter.

The winter air is very, very cold. A parka helps keep each person warm. It is made from animal skin and fur.

Boots are yanked on every day. They keep out water and snow. They, too, are made of animal skin and are very warm.

The Inuit use special gear to travel across the ice and snow. They used sleds for many years, but now they use snowmobiles too.

Life in the cold Arctic is not easy.
But the Inuit know how to live there
and survive. They enjoy their special,
splendid home.